THE TROUBLES IN NORTHERN IRELAND

IVAN MINNIS

Heinemann
LIBRARY

www.heinemann.co.uk
Visit our website to find out more information about **Heinemann Library** books.

To order:
 Phone 44 (0) 1865 888066
 Send a fax to 44 (0) 1865 314091
 Visit the Heinemann Bookshop at www.heinemann.co.uk to browse our catalogue
and order online.

First published in Great Britain by Heinemann Library, Halley Court, Jordan Hill, Oxford
OX2 8EJ, a division of Reed Educational and Professional Publishing Ltd.
Heinemann is a registered trademark of Reed Educational and Professional Publishing Ltd.

OXFORD MELBOURNE AUCKLAND JOHANNESBURG BLANTYRE GABORONE
IBADAN PORTSMOUTH (NH) USA CHICAGO

© Reed Educational and Professional Publishing Ltd 2001
The moral right of the proprietor has been asserted.

Designed by AMR
Illustrated by Chartwell Illustrators
Originated by Dot Gradations
Printed by South China Printers

05 04 03 02   05 04 03 02
10 9 8 7 6 5 4 3 2   10 9 8 7 6 5 4 3 2 1
ISBN 0 431 11862 0 (hardback)   ISBN 0 431 11868 X (paperback)

British Library Cataloguing in Publication Data

Minnis, Ivan
  The troubles in Northern Ireland. – (Troubled world)
  1. Northern Ireland – Politics and government – 1969-1994 – Juvenile literature 2. Northern
  Ireland – Politics and government – 1994- – Juvenile literature
  I. Title
  941.6'0824

Acknowledgements
The publishers would like to thank the following for permission to reproduce photographs:
Pg.7 Hulton Getty; Pg.8 Hulton Getty; Pg.9 Hulton Getty; Pg.11 Hulton Getty; Pg.12 Hulton
Getty; Pg.14 Rex Features; Pg.17 Rex Features; Pg.19 Popperfoto; Pg.22 Victor Patterson
Archive/Linen Hall; Pg.23 Hulton Getty; Pg.25 Popperfoto; Pg.26 Popperfoto; Pg.27 Popperfoto;
Pg.28 Victor Patterson Archive/Linen Hall; Pg.31 Victor Patterson Archive/Linen Hall; Pg.32 Peter
Marlow/Magnum; Pg.33 Popperfoto; Pg.34 Gilles Peress/Magnum; Pg.36 Hulton Getty; Pg.37
Popperfoto; Pg.39 Rex Features; Pg.41 [top] Rex Features [bottom] Popperfoto; Pg.42 Rex
Features; Pg.43 Corbis; Pg.44 *Belfast Telegraph*; Pg.45 *Daily Mail*; Pg.46 Pearson Television Stills
Library; Pg.49 Rex Features; Pg.51 Rex Features; Pg.54 Popperfoto/Reuters; Pg.55
Popperfoto/Reuters; Pg.56 Popperfoto; Pg.58 Rex Features.

Cover photograph reproduced with permission of Topham Picturepoint.

Every effort has been made to contact copyright holders of any material reproduced in this
book. Any omissions will be rectified in subsequent printings if notice is given to the publishers.

Contents

Words that appear in the text in bold, **like this**, are explained in the glossary.

A Divided Society

Until 1969 Northern Ireland rarely made the front pages of the world's press. It was, and remains, a small part of a small island on the fringes of Europe. It has a population of around 1.7 million, mainly living in rural communities and small towns dotted across some of Ireland's most beautiful countryside. Its capital, Belfast, and its second city, Londonderry, appear like any other industrial towns, buzzing with shoppers and nightlife. However, in their centres and side streets, and on the country roads of the rest of the **province**, hundreds of people have been killed or maimed over the past 30 years.

The Irish province of **Ulster** originally occupied nine counties in the north of Ireland. Northern Ireland is made up of six of these: Antrim, Down, Fermanagh, Londonderry, Tyrone and Armagh. With only two major towns, much of the population is employed in agriculture or serving the rural communities. The heavy industry in the cities has crumbled in the face of economic competition and the problems of attracting investment to such an unstable region. As a result, Northern Ireland suffers from high unemployment, particularly in the west of the province, and from the emigration of its young people.

The people of Northern Ireland have been torn apart by 400 years of religious and political quarrels, culminating in 30 years of violence since 1969. The 'troubles', as this latest outbreak of violence has become known, have led to the deaths of over 3500 people, and have driven a wedge between the majority community, the **Protestants**, and their **Catholic** neighbours. The 1991 **census** in Northern Ireland found that most people lived in areas more than 90 per cent Protestant or Catholic. Children attend segregated schools, grow up separately and rarely socialize together as adults.

Such division may seem extreme, but it is deep rooted. Flags are hoisted along quiet country roads and through residential areas, The **Unionist** Protestants fly the Union Jack or Northern Irish Flag, while Catholic **Nationalists** fly the Irish Tricolour. Kerbstones are painted in the colours of one or other flag, and the banners and names of **paramilitary** groups ensure that all visitors know who controls the area.

The troubles have grown out of this division and the mistrust which feeds off it, but they have had effects far beyond the streets of Northern Ireland. Bombs have been exploded in England and the Irish **Republic** and attacks have been carried out across Europe as paramilitary groups have attempted to influence politicians and attract publicity to their cause.

What's in a name?

The importance of symbolism extends to the name of Northern Ireland's second city, Londonderry, or Derry. London Merchants were granted the area around the ancient settlement of Doire (Derry) during the plantation (see pages 6–9). They rebuilt and fortified the town, renaming it Londonderry. In modern times the name of the town has caused controversy. Catholics use the name Derry, objecting to the British and plantation connections of the more recent name. The Nationalist controlled council changed its name to Derry City Council in 1984. Unionists continue to use Londonderry. As a result of this dilemma television news bulletins in Northern Ireland use the two names alternately, to avoid causing offence to either community. In the interests of impartiality this book will do the same.

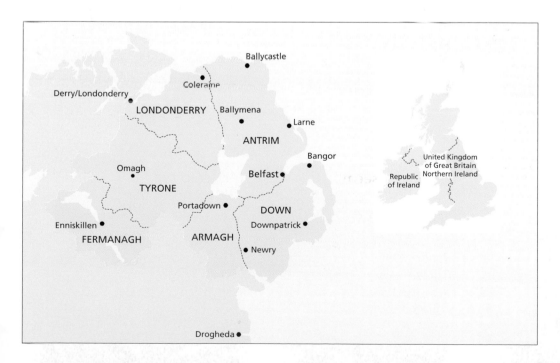

The Origins of Conflict

Observers of the present conflict in Northern Ireland are often surprised at the influence of events that occurred long ago in the past. Key speeches are made at rallies commemorating rebellions and battles that seem, to the outsider, to have little relevance to the present day. The attitudes and beliefs of each side are the result of centuries of mistrust and conflict, not just the consequence of the past 30 years.

The Plantation of Ulster

England's involvement in Irish politics and history goes back over 1000 years, but the most crucial event in the creation of the two communities in Northern Ireland took place 400 years ago. During the reign of Elizabeth I, Ireland had become an increasingly troublesome part of her realm. The English feared that Spain would use **Catholic** Ireland as a stepping-stone for invasion, so it was decided to introduce **Protestant** settlers into **Ulster**. These settlers, it was hoped, would make Ulster peaceful and loyal to the English crown. Many of the Protestants in Ulster today can trace their ancestry back to these settlers.

Needless to say the native Irish did not take kindly to these new arrivals. Resentment grew and exploded into violence in 1641. Over 10,000 Protestant settlers were killed in the first brutal months of the rebellion, with this figure greatly exaggerated by English writers. In 1649 Oliver Cromwell arrived to put down the rebels and take revenge for the events of 1641: he captured the town of Drogheda, killing nearly 3000 people. The events of the 1640s sowed seeds of mistrust and hatred in the minds of both communities in Ulster.

The Williamite Wars

Ireland again became a centre for violent conflict in the late 17th century. Religious tension in England led to the replacement of the Catholic King James II by the Dutch Protestant William III, with Ireland as their battleground. In 1688 King James's forces laid siege to Derry, at that time filled with Protestant **planters** fearing a repeat of the events of 1641. The siege lasted for 105 days and brought great suffering to the city's population before relief eventually arrived. The following year saw a resounding victory for King William's forces at the Battle of the Boyne and James was exiled to France.

The events of these years were to have far reaching consequences for the people of Ireland. Today the summer months resound to the beat of drums as the Protestant **Orange Order** and **Apprentice Boys** take to the streets to remember the Siege and the Battle of the Boyne. These marches are regarded by Unionists as central to their culture, but have at times resulted in street violence.

The 1798 rebellion

King William's victory led to a Protestant dominance of Irish politics for the next century. The Penal Laws, enacted between 1697 and 1727, stated that land bequeathed by Catholics had to be divided equally among the sons of the family, unless one son agreed to become a Protestant. They could not receive an education or become MPs. **Presbyterians** also suffered under the Penal Laws that gave a special position to the **Anglican** Church.

The Presbyterians and the Catholics became allied during the United Irishmen rebellion of 1798 which was led by Theobald Wolfe Tone, a Presbyterian lawyer from Dublin. The rebellion was doomed to failure: early successes were lost as Catholic massacres of Protestants in the south alienated their Presbyterian allies in the north.

Despite the failure of the rebellion, its effects are still felt today. The modern **Republican** movement traces its ancestry back to the United Irishmen. In 1800, the Act of Union was introduced, bringing Ireland directly under the control of the British. Presbyterians saw their position in society improved and turned to the Anglican community for political allies: Irish Unionism was born.

**A Republican icon:
Theobald Wolfe Tone.**

Members of the Ulster Volunteer Force in training during the Home Rule crisis.

The Home Rule crisis

The 19th century saw great changes in Ireland. Unionism strengthened as the north became increasingly industrialized and linked to trade with the British Empire. Erosion of the Penal Laws extended the vote to **Catholics**, who campaigned for Irish self-government. The potato famine of 1845–49 saw millions starve or emigrate, increasing anti-British feeling. Thus, as the century drew to a close, there were two firmly entrenched camps: **Unionists** wanting to protect their links with Britain; **Nationalists** arguing for self-government.

From this period of turmoil emerged the Northern Ireland State. Catholic Nationalists moved away from trying to gain total independence for Ireland and instead started to seek limited self-government, known as Home Rule. The **Protestant** Unionists, mainly concentrated in the industrial northern **province** of **Ulster**, were concerned that their prosperity and religion would suffer in a mainly agricultural and Catholic Irish state.

Unionists and their Conservative Party allies in London were able to hold off two attempts to introduce Home Rule, but the crisis reached its height after the successful passage of the Third Home Rule Bill in 1912. This guaranteed Ireland Home Rule within two years. Unionists made plans to rule Ulster separately and formed their own army to back them up. The Ulster Volunteer Force (UVF) was a well-trained and equipped body of about 100,000 men. They hoped to be able to force the Liberal government to change their plans. Meanwhile, Nationalists formed their own force, the Irish Volunteers, to make sure that the government would think twice before **repealing** Home Rule.

By 1914, Ireland seemed to be on the brink of civil war. However, the outbreak of the First World War meant that Home Rule was shelved. By the end of the war events in Dublin had made Home Rule irrelevant.

The Easter Rising 1916

Although Irish Nationalism had turned towards the peaceful campaign for Home Rule, there remained a small number of **Republicans** who were ready to use violence to achieve full independence for Ireland. They saw the war, with the British distracted by more important matters in Europe, as providing a chance for Ireland to gain her freedom. The rebels, led by the poet and schoolteacher Patrick Pearse, failed to take power. However, their subsequent executions inspired a revival of Republicanism. The general election of 1918 saw a massive defeat for the old Home Rule Party, as Nationalists flocked to vote for Sinn Féin, its Republican successor.

War and partition

A brutal War of Independence followed, with the reorganized Irish Volunteers becoming The Irish Republican Army (IRA). The war was brought to an end with the Anglo-Irish Treaty of 1921. Ireland was to be divided, with the six counties of Northern Ireland remaining part of the United Kingdom. Britain retained some say in the government of the southern 26 counties, which became known as the Irish Free State. In the north the Unionists reluctantly accepted that six counties was all that they could hope to control. However, the Free State descended into civil war. Pro-Treaty forces regarded the deal as the best they could hope for but others saw it as betrayal of the principles behind the Easter Rising. The pro-treaty forces emerged victorious, and Ireland settled into relative peace. Sporadic IRA campaigns against **partition** continued but little changed until the North erupted into violence in the late 1960s.

Dublin during the Easter Rising, 1916.

9

Taking Sides: Unionism and Nationalism

In most **democratic** countries people often change the political party they vote for at elections, even if this means a great change in how the country will be ruled. It is different in Northern Ireland: most people consider themselves to be either **Nationalists** or **Unionists** and, in doing so, are saying which state they think should rule the country, not just how it should be ruled. While there is movement of voters between the various political parties within Unionism or Nationalism, few change their loyalty from one to the other.

Unionism

Unionists mainly come from the **Protestant** community. Many are descended from Scottish and English immigrants who came to **Ulster** during the 17th century plantation. They now form the majority of the population of Northern Ireland. They wish to keep the links between Northern Ireland and Great Britain that were set up under the Act of Union of 1800.

Arguments for the Union

Prosperity: Traditionally, Ulster was the most industrial part of Ireland and Unionists feared that the loss of links with Britain would lead to a loss in prosperity. As the industries of Northern Ireland declined, Unionists argued that the United Kingdom offered the better social services and opportunities for economic development.

Religion: Unionists fear that the **Catholic** Church would dominate an all-Ireland state and that their beliefs would be ignored. They argue that the Protestant community in the south declined dramatically after **partition** and that the same would happen in a united Ireland.

Culture: Unionists are very proud of their British citizenship and regard themselves as being different from the rest of the people of Ireland. The huge **Orange Order** marches which take place on 12 July symbolize this cultural difference and loyalty to the United Kingdom.

Unionist Political Parties:

The Ulster Unionist Party. The UUP is the largest of Northern Ireland's political parties. It is the more moderate of the two main Unionist parties and has shown itself willing to share power with Nationalists and **Republicans**. At the time of publication it is led by David Trimble.

The Democratic Unionist Party. The DUP was formed in 1971 by the Reverend Ian Paisley, who, at the time of publication, remains its leader. His supporters were unhappy with the UUP's more moderate policies. They have been opposed to sharing power with Nationalists, especially Sinn Féin, the representatives of the IRA.

The Orange Order. Although not a political party, the Orange Order has a great deal of influence over Unionist politics. It was formed in 1795 to defend Protestant areas and its membership of around 100,000 is entirely Protestant.

Ian Paisley addresses an early political meeting, 1969.

Nationalism

Nationalists are mainly drawn from the minority **Catholic** community, many descending from the native population who lived in **Ulster** before the plantation. They hope that Ireland will be united and independent of Britain. Unlike the more extreme **Republicans** (see pages 14–17), they aim to bring about a united Ireland using peaceful methods.

Arguments for a United Ireland

Prosperity: Nationalists believe that British control in Ireland has held back its economy. They feel that Britain has treated Ireland like a **colony** and if the Irish had complete control there would be better economic development.

Religion: Many Catholics in Northern Ireland feel that the majority **Protestant** community has treated them as second-class citizens. They say that the Irish constitution protects all religions so Protestants have nothing to fear in a united Ireland.

Culture: Most of the Catholic community regard themselves as Irish citizens. They feel that Irish identity, language, sports and music are stifled by British involvement.

John Hume, leader of the SDLP since 1979.

Nationalist Political Parties

The main Nationalist party in Northern Ireland is the Social Democratic and Labour Party (SDLP). Formed in 1970, it has been led by John Hume since 1979. It is opposed to IRA violence and hopes to share power with all parties in Northern Ireland.

The Centre Ground

Many in Northern Ireland feel that the argument over **partition** has stopped discussion of more important issues. They believe that Protestants and Catholics should work together to solve the problems of unemployment and social deprivation. Even for many who would describe themselves as **Unionist** or Nationalist, these issues are more important than partition.

Political Parties

The Alliance Party was founded in 1970 and attracts members and votes from both communities. Although it favours the union, it hopes to encourage Protestants and Catholics to come together to run Northern Ireland.

The *1991* **census** *figures* show that 38.4% of the population regarded themselves as Catholic; 50.6% Protestant and other; 3.7% professed no religion; 7.3% gave no response.

The *British Social Attitudes Surveys* in 1991 and 1993 asked the people of Northern Ireland for their constitutional preferences:

	Protestant		Catholic	
Constitutional preference	*1991*	*1993*	*1991*	*1993*
Remain part of the United Kingdom	92%	90%	35%	36%
Become part of a united Ireland	4%	5%	53%	49%

Taking Sides: Republicans and Loyalists

Some people within each community in Northern Ireland believe that peaceful methods alone are unlikely to achieve their aims. Extremists on each side – **Republicans** from the **Nationalist** community; **Loyalists** from within Unionism – have used violence to attempt to force change.

Republicans

Republicans want a united, independent Ireland but believe that this is unlikely to come about purely through peaceful methods. They regard themselves as the descendants of the leaders of the Easter Rising and that their 'armed struggle' is a continuance of the War of Independence. They see the British Army as 'an army of occupation' and are prepared to use violence to force them to withdraw. Members of the **Royal Ulster Constabulary (RUC)** and the **Protestant** community are also targeted, as they are regarded as being supporters of British rule.

Martin McGuinness (left) and Gerry Adams at the finale of a Sinn Féin Party conference.

Private Armies

The Irish Republican Army (IRA) was formed in 1919. It continued its struggle against the British after **partition**, with failed campaigns in the 1940s and 50s. When street violence erupted in 1969 the IRA was unprepared and poorly equipped. It soon split into the 'Official' and 'Provisional' IRA, with the Officials abandoning violence in the early 1970s. The Provisionals continued a campaign of bombings and shootings in an attempt to force a British withdrawal, until a ceasefire was called in 1995, to allow the talks that have led to the peace process. The ceasefire ended with the Canary Wharf bomb of February 1996 but a second ceasefire, which has held, was announced in July the following year.

The Irish National Liberation Army (INLA) split off from the IRA in the early 1970s. It is a small but ruthless organization that aims to create an all-Ireland **Socialist Republic**. It too has called a ceasefire, although it does not feel that the present peace process will succeed. It has a small political wing called the Irish Republican Socialist Party.

The Real IRA and the Continuity IRA split off from the main Republican movement in opposition to the ceasefires. They are small but capable of carrying out devastating attacks, such as the Omagh bombing of 1998.

Political Parties

Sinn Féin is a legal political party with close links to the IRA. In the 1980s it began to put forward candidates in local and national elections although its MPs refuse to take their seats in Westminster. Widespread sympathy for the **hunger strikers** (see pages 32–5) allowed it to gain support in many Nationalist areas in the early 1980s. This success encouraged many within the party to feel that gains could be made through politics rather than violence, leading to the IRA ceasefire of 1995. It is led by Gerry Adams, one of the party's two MPs.

Loyalists

Loyalist paramilitary groups emerged in the 1960s and early 1970s, claiming to be the defenders of **Protestant** areas. They believe that the army and **RUC** are unable to deal with IRA violence and they aim to hit back at **Republicans**. Members of the wider **Catholic** community have also been targeted, as the Loyalist paramilitaries feel that they support and protect the IRA.

Private Armies

The Ulster Volunteer Force (UVF) was set up in the 1960s, taking its name from the force formed to resist Home Rule in 1912. It is the smaller of the two main Loyalist paramilitary groups and has been on ceasefire since 1995. Some members were opposed to this move and formed the Loyalist Volunteer Force (LVF), which continued with violence until it too declared a ceasefire in 1998.

The Ulster Defence Association (UDA) is the largest Loyalist paramilitary group. It was formed in 1971 to defend Protestant areas during riots. It remained legal until the early 1980s, with its acts of violence carried out under the name of the Ulster Freedom Fighters (UFF). It joined the UVF on ceasefire in 1995.

Political Parties

The representatives of Loyalist paramilitary groups have not attracted the same level of political support as the Republican movement.

The Progressive Unionist Party (PUP), led by David Ervine, are the political representatives of the UVF. It has attracted some support in parts of Belfast but remains relatively small, with only two seats in the Northern Ireland Assembly, having gained 3.5 per cent of the total vote.

The Ulster Democratic Party (UDP) represents the UDA. It failed to win any seats in the assembly elections but has several local councillors, including its leader, Gary McMichael.

The IRA bombing of Enniskillen, that killed eleven innocent people, in November 1987 angered and shocked members of both the Protestant and Catholic communities.

Thirty years of violence

Three thousand, six hundred and thirty-six people were killed and thousands more wounded and maimed between 1966 and 1999. Republican paramilitaries have been responsible for 2139 of the deaths linked to the troubles. Loyalist paramilitaries have killed 1050 with the security forces accounting for 367. The conflict has often degenerated into 'tit-for-tat' violence with either side responding to the other's attacks.

One month of violence: July 1976

The month began with the shootings of an English tourist and a Catholic by Loyalists and ended with the murder of nine in a car bomb attack on the village of Claudy in Co. Derry by the IRA: five of them Protestants, the rest Catholics. In total 96 people died as a result of the spiralling violence, the youngest just five months old, the oldest 71. Loyalists killed 25, Republicans 51 and the British Army 19, with one murder unclaimed. Although that month was particularly bloody – in the 1970s no year surpassed that figure – in many ways it is representative of the troubles. Loyalist and Republican paramilitaries were killed, as were members of the security forces, but the majority were civilians from both communities.

Northern Ireland and the Wider World

The Irish American connection and NORAID

The Irish Famine of 1845–49 led to the emigration of around one million people, fleeing poverty and starvation. This emigration continued for the next 150 years as people left in search of a better life. The vast proportion of these emigrants went to America. As a result there is a huge Irish-American population that is both sympathetic to the **Nationalist** cause and powerful in American politics.

The **Republican** movement has always had willing listeners among the Irish-American community. In the 19th century organizations such as the Fenian movement and Clan-na-Gael were prominent in providing men and money for militant Republicans in Ireland. With the onset of the present troubles, the Northern Aid Committee (NORAID) was set up and has been able to raise millions of dollars. NORAID claims that the money raised was intended to support the families of imprisoned Republicans rather than purchase weapons but many Irish and Irish-American leaders dispute this.

American politicians and Ireland

John Hume of the SDLP has been instrumental in bringing the Northern Ireland issue to the forefront of American politics. Irish-American Senators such as Edward Kennedy have argued that Britain's presence in Ireland should come to an end but have maintained that violence is not the way to achieve this. American Presidents have tried to avoid such direct demands for a British withdrawal, aware of the importance of Britain's involvement in NATO.

It is during the present peace process that Irish-America has become central to Northern Irish politics. Pressure from Irish-America helped bring about the first IRA ceasefire and President Clinton made the issue central to his foreign policy. Clinton's regular meetings with both **Unionist** and Nationalist leaders have helped break political stalemates. Senator George Mitchell, who chaired the talks which led to the Good Friday Agreement, has also been a well-respected and influential figure in the peace process. Many Unionists however are mistrustful of Irish-American involvement in the peace process, feeling that they favour the Nationalists and Republicans.

Global terrorism?

The IRA has also been successful in developing links and attracting support from some of the USA's most bitter enemies. Colonel Gadaffi's regime in Libya has been a major source of weapons for the Republican movement, a fact made clear when 150 tonnes of Libyan weapons bound for the IRA were seized in November 1987. The IRA also has supporters elsewhere in the Arab world such as the Palestine Liberation Organisation (PLO), and the Basque separatist group ETA in Spain.

Unionists

Unionist politicians have not had the benefit of such a huge body of potential support as Irish-America. The **Orange Order** has a substantial membership around the world, most notably in Canada and Scotland but its strength is declining. Unionists have therefore looked mainly to the UK for support, especially within their traditional allies, the Conservative Party.

Loyalist paramilitaries

Loyalists have had greater difficulty finding supplies of weapons than their Republican counterparts. They have been able to gain limited supplies from sympathizers in Canada and Scotland but have mainly relied on the much riskier source of illegal arms.

American government policy in Northern Ireland
'Violence cannot resolve Northern Ireland's problems: it only increases them and solves nothing ... US government policy on the Northern Ireland issue has long been one of impartiality and that is how it will remain.'
President Carter, August 1977

David Trimble, leader of the Ulster Unionists, holding talks with President Clinton.

Turning Point: Civil Rights

From it's creation in 1921, Northern Ireland was ruled by the **Unionist** Party. The state had a built-in Unionist majority that ensured the **Catholic Nationalists** had no hope of achieving either power or a say in how the country was run. Unionists justified this on the grounds that Nationalists were opposed to the existence of the Northern Ireland state and therefore were not entitled to any say in its operation. They pointed to continued IRA violence as evidence that Nationalists wanted to destroy Northern Ireland.

In 1963, however, a new Unionist Prime Minister came into power. Captain Terence O'Neill promised reforms in the allocation of housing, the education system and the voting system to ensure Catholics got a fairer deal. In 1965 he met the Irish **Taoiseach**, Sean Lemass, in Belfast to discuss cross-border economic co-operation: the first meeting of the leaders of the two parts of Ireland. This seemed to indicate a new era in Irish politics, but soon O'Neill was under fire from both Unionists and Nationalists in the North.

Unionist objections: the influence of the Reverend Ian Paisley

Some Unionists were concerned at the growing relationship with the **Republic**. In particular, the supporters of the Reverend Ian Paisley objected to the involvement of the Republic in the affairs of Northern Ireland. They pointed to Articles 2 and 3 of the Republic's Constitution, which laid claim to Northern Ireland and to the special position that the Catholic Church held in the southern state. When O'Neill met the new Taoiseach Jack Lynch in early 1967 the atmosphere in the **province** was tense. The previous year had seen an increase in **sectarian** tension as Nationalists celebrated the 50th anniversary of the Easter Rising and Unionists remembered their losses at the Battle of the Somme. There were immediate demands for O'Neill's resignation with Paisley's supporters accusing him of being a new Colonel Lundy – the Governor of Londonderry before the siege of 1688–89 who had advised surrender to King James' forces – because O'Neill was surrendering to **Ulster's** modern enemies.

Nationalist objections: the rise of the Civil Rights movement

For many among the Nationalist population O'Neill was too slow in delivering his promised reforms and they did not go far enough. The Northern Ireland **Civil Rights** Association (NICRA) was set up in 1967. Based on the American movement for Civil Rights led by Martin Luther King, it addressed what it regarded as practices that discriminated against Catholics and called for:

Elections

- The introduction of the 'one-man-one-vote' principal for elections. (At the time only property owners could vote in local government elections, in some areas these were mainly wealthier **Protestants**.)
- The end of **gerrymandering**, which allowed Unionists to control Catholic areas by fixing electoral boundaries.

Jobs and Housing

- Fair play for Catholics in public housing allocation.
- An end to discrimination in government jobs.
- A complaints procedure against local government.

Law and Order

- The disbandment of the **B-Specials** (a reserve police force, almost entirely Protestant, set up in the 1920s to deal with IRA violence).
- The abolition of the Special Powers Act, which allowed the police wide-ranging powers to deal with violence and opposition to the state.

Housing conditions: a Catholic view

'(There were) appalling slum conditions in Derry and yet people just couldn't get houses. They had to live in converted army huts. They had to live a couple of families to a house and so on.'
Michel Farrell, a leader of People's Democracy *(an offshoot of NICRA)*

A Protestant view

*'Our housing was the same as our **Catholic** next-door neighbour – two up and two-down with an outside toilet. It irks me when I hear about the disadvantages that the Catholics had and the agenda for equality that they go on about now.'*
Bobby Norris, an ex-Loyalist Paramilitary

Feelings run high as Civil Rights Association protestors march in Co. Tyrone.

Marches and riots

The **Civil Rights** Association adopted the tactics of their American and French contemporaries. Marches were organized to draw the attention of the London government to the position of **Catholics** in Northern Ireland. In October 1968 a banned Civil Rights march in Derry was followed by violence between marchers and the police, with violent images flashed around the world. Pressure on O'Neill began to grow and he was forced to concede some of the demands of the movement.

The fall of O'Neill

O'Neill's promised reforms were broadly accepted by NICRA but did not go far enough for some **Nationalists**, and went too far for some **Unionists**. Crucially for some civil rights activists, he failed to address the principle of 'one man one vote'. A further march was organized by the 'People's Democracy', an offshoot of NICRA, between Belfast and Derry in January of 1969. The marchers hoped to provoke a reaction from Paisley's supporters that would further highlight their cause in London. They were not disappointed; the march was met with a vicious attack by Unionist protesters, including off-duty **B-Specials** at Burntollet in Co. Londonderry, and further rioting followed in Derry City that night.

O'Neill now had little choice but to call an election to seek support for his reforms, but with only limited success. Paisley's supporters claimed that O'Neill was giving in to NICRA, which to them was merely a cover for **Republicans** and the IRA. Arousing such fears, they were able to split the Unionist vote enough to severely weaken O'Neill's position. Soon after this, having failed to gain support for the introduction of 'one man one vote', O'Neill was forced to resign.

The arrival of British troops

Violence erupted across Northern Ireland throughout the summer of 1969 as Nationalists fought police and B-Specials. The **Apprentice Boys** parade in Londonderry on 12 August was followed by fierce fighting between Catholics and the police in what became known as 'the Battle of the Bogside.' The violence spread to Belfast as Nationalists attempted to stretch the police to help their counterparts in Derry. The tactic succeeded: on 15 August, Prime Minister Harold Wilson ordered in British troops to relieve the **Royal Ulster Constabulary** in what was intended to be a temporary measure. At first welcomed by the Catholic population, who regarded them as protection from the mainly **Protestant** RUC, the army soon found itself under fire as more **militant** Nationalism emerged.

British troops patrolling the streets of Belfast, 1972.

Turning Point: Bloody Sunday and the Fall of Stormont

Between 1969 and 1971 the situation gradually worsened. In 1970 the IRA split into the 'Official' and 'Provisional' branches. The latter was a more **militant** and violent organization that found willing recruits among a **Catholic** population who felt threatened by increasing **sectarian** violence. The Provisionals raised the stakes with a campaign of bombings and shootings; **Protestant paramilitary** groups increased their activities in response. The security situation spiralled out of control: 1971 saw the deaths of 174 people, compared to 25 the previous year.

Internment

By mid 1971 it was evident that the army and police were not able to deal with the increased paramilitary activity. Heavy-handed army tactics in Catholic areas had alienated the local population. They regarded the arms searches and raids on houses as being directed solely towards their community while Protestant violence continued unchecked. This feeling was intensified in August when the **Unionist** government introduced 'internment' in an attempt to relieve the pressure on the army and **RUC**.

Internment gave the police the power to arrest and detain without trial anyone suspected of IRA involvement. It had been used to good effect on both sides of the border against the IRA campaign of 1956–62 but in ten years crucial factors had changed. The Irish government was not prepared to support its northern neighbour, as sympathy grew for the IRA in the south. Thus suspects were able to find sanctuary over the border and outdated RUC intelligence meant that few members of the Provisionals were actually detained.

Internment also failed to address **Loyalist** paramilitaries, increasing the sense of hostility felt among the Catholic population. Far from reducing violence, more people than ever were killed, and internment became a new target for **civil rights** marches and protests.

Bloody Sunday

One of these marches was organized for Londonderry in January 1972. The government banned it fearing violence, but the march itself passed off peacefully. However, as the crowd dispersed youths began to shower stones on the army, who replied with water cannon and rubber bullets. What happened next remains a matter of controversy. Soldiers of the Parachute Regiment opened fire upon the crowd and in the resulting mayhem 13 people were killed, with another subsequently dying of his injuries.

Afterwards the army claimed that their men had been fired upon from the crowd but relatives of the dead maintain that the only shots fired came from the army themselves. The resulting Widgery Tribunal, set up to find the truth about the events, concluded that the army was fired upon, but that none of the dead had been armed. The conclusions have been the subject of controversy for 30 years as it was stated that the deaths were the responsibility of the march organizers. Many **Nationalists** regarded the Tribunal as biased, aimed at deflecting criticism from the British army. A prolonged campaign to re-examine the events finally met with success in April 2000 with the opening of the Saville enquiry.

Bloody Sunday, January 1972. Thirteen die when British troops fire on protestors.

Angry Unionists protest at the imposition of direct rule from Westminster.

Direct Rule

Bloody Sunday sparked a rapid increase in violence as the IRA exacted revenge for the killings. **Loyalists** responded in kind and many began to fear that Northern Ireland was about to descend into civil war. The Prime Minister of Northern Ireland, Brian Faulkner, asked to be allowed to introduce new security measures. The British Prime Minister, Edward Heath, refused. He insisted that the Westminster government should have total control of security matters, something that Faulkner and his colleagues could not accept. In March 1972 Heath decided to introduce direct rule from Westminster. The Northern Ireland parliament at Stormont was suspended and a Secretary of State took control of the day-to-day running of the **province**.

Unionists were furious. They regarded the removal of their parliament as a betrayal: another concession to the **Republican** movement. A new Loyalist **paramilitary** group was formed, the **Ulster** Defence Association, and **sectarian** murders increased. Republicans, on the other hand, did not regard direct rule as any concession to them. Bitterness after Bloody Sunday combined with anger about a greater role for Britain in Ireland's affairs led to an increase in IRA violence. 1972 saw the deaths of 477 people in Northern Ireland with thousands injured. The British government, having held fruitless talks with the IRA, began to look at power-sharing as a potential solution.

Bloody Sunday

'There would have been no deaths in Londonderry on 30 January if those who had organized an illegal march had not ... created a highly dangerous situation in which a clash between demonstrators and the security forces was almost inevitable ... each soldier was his own judge of whether he had identified a gunman'
The Widgery Report, 18 April 1972

'... at one stage a lone army sniper fired two shots at me as I peered around a corner. People could be seen moving forward ... their hands above their heads. One man was carrying a white handkerchief. Gunfire was directed even at them and they fled or fell to the ground.'
Simon Winchester, a journalist writing in The Guardian, 31 January 1971

A modern mural in Derry's Bogside commemorating Bloody Sunday.

Sunningdale and the Ulster Workers Strike

New political parties

The late 1960s and early 1970s saw an increasing disillusionment with the old political establishment in Northern Ireland. New political parties began to emerge to challenge them, both on the street and in elections. In 1970 the Social **Democratic** and Labour Party (SDLP) replaced the **Nationalist** Party, which had represented the **Catholic** community in Stormont. The **Unionist** Party, after 50 years in power, began to lose its grip on the **Protestant** community. The Alliance Party was formed to provide a platform for more liberal Unionists who hoped for a closer relationship with the Nationalist community. More extreme elements moved to Ian Paisley's Democratic Unionist Party (DUP) and William Craig's Vanguard. This fracturing of the Unionists was to have important consequences for the attempts to find a solution to the growing crisis.

The Social Democratic and Labour Party emerged from the political turmoil of the early 1970's as a replacement for the mainly Catholic Nationalist Party.

Power-sharing

The increase in violence led the British government to search for a solution which would isolate the **paramilitaries**. They hoped to persuade democratic Nationalists and Unionists to work together in an assembly, with a **consultative body** to involve the Dublin government. In March 1973, their plans met with a cautious welcome from the leader of the Unionist Party, Brian Faulkner.

Other Unionists opposed the proposed power-sharing assembly, which led to the formation of Vanguard. In the resulting election of June 1973 there was a clear majority in favour of the new power-sharing assembly. However, the splintering of Unionism meant Faulkner's pro-assembly group held fewer seats than the anti-assembly Unionists.

A Power-sharing **Executive** was set up with seven 'Official' (pro-assembly) Unionists, six SDLP and two Alliance members. The anti-assembly Unionists refused to take part, arguing that the SDLP's goal of a united Ireland should exclude them from government. This, combined with the fact that the future role of the Republic had not yet been decided, ensured that a number of problems remained.

Party	Seats	Percentage of Votes
Pro-assembly Unionist	24	29
Anti-assembly Unionist*	26	33
SDLP	19	22
Alliance Party	8	9
NI Labour Party	1	3

*DUP 8, Vanguard 7, West Belfast **Loyalists** 3, 'unpledged' Unionists 8. Sinn Féin gained around three per cent of the vote, but no seats.

The Sunningdale Agreement

The 'Irish dimension' to the agreement had to be arranged before the new Power-sharing Executive could be put into action. A conference was held at Sunningdale in Berkshire, with delegates from the British and Irish governments and the pro-assembly leaders from Northern Ireland. It was agreed that a Council of Ireland should be created which would have 'executive and harmonizing functions and a consultative role'. It would consist of a Council of Ministers, with seven members of the NI executive, seven Irish ministers and 30 members each from the NI Assembly and the Irish Dáil. Surprisingly, Faulkner agreed to the Republic's involvement in the affairs of the North concluding that it was merely a consultative body that had no real power. Nationalists and the Irish government, however, regarded it as an opportunity to gradually increase cross-border links.

The Power-sharing Executive

The Power-sharing **Executive** took office in January 1974, but any optimism for its chances of success soon disappeared as the difficulties began to emerge. Anti-agreement **Unionists** had been excluded from the Sunningdale conference and had refused to take part in the Executive itself. They immediately joined forces, calling themselves the United **Ulster** Unionist Council (UUUC). They began to disrupt the work of the Assembly and criticized Faulkner for his acceptance of the Council of Ireland. Faulkner was not helped by the fact that the role of the Council was unclear, so his Unionist opponents were able to use the evidence of **Nationalist** support to argue that the Executive would lead to a united Ireland.

Faulkner came under increasing pressure within his own party. He was forced to resign as leader when his Westminster MPs declared their support for the pro-UUUC Harry West. February 1974 saw a British general election. Faulkner's Unionists were utterly defeated. UUUC candidates won eleven of the twelve Westminster seats, polling 51 per cent of the vote while Faulkner's supporters could manage only thirteen per cent. Despite this the assembly limped on with Faulkner at its head, but it was soon to be dealt a crushing blow.

The Ulster Workers' strike

In late 1973 the Ulster Workers' Council (UWC) was formed by a group of **Protestant** Trade Unionists prepared to take strike action to oppose any government plans they found unacceptable. After the fall of Faulkner many Unionists called for fresh assembly elections to overthrow his Executive, and the Council of Ireland. When this was refused, on 14 May, the UWC called a General Strike. It soon became clear that their threat to bring Northern Ireland to a standstill was serious as they controlled the electricity supplies and could prevent the distribution of petrol. They also had the support of the majority of Unionists.

'(Power-sharing was) nothing less than the first instalment and down payment on an eventual united Ireland scheme.'
Ian Paisely, Protestant Unionist, Leader of the Democratic Unionist Party, 23 November 1973

The British government was unwilling to negotiate with the strikers and attempts to organize a return to work failed in the face of the well-coordinated UWC. They were assisted in their efforts by the might of the Ulster Defence Association (UDA) who ensured that anyone who might wish to cross picket lines would think twice. After ten days of strike action the Prime Minister, Harold Wilson, described the strikers as 'people who spend their lives sponging on… British Democracy.' Unionists were outraged, and support for the strike became almost total within the Protestant community.

Faulkner was in an impossible position and asked the Secretary of State to negotiate with the strikers. The government remained opposed to this so Faulkner and his fellow Unionist members of the Executive resigned and power-sharing was brought to an end. Victorious, the UWC called an end to the strike and Northern Ireland returned to direct rule from Westminster.

Working class Protestants celebrate at the collapse of the Power-sharing Executive in 1974.

Turning Point: The Hunger Strike

The failure of the 1974 Power-sharing **Executive** left a vacuum at the centre of the politics of Northern Ireland which successive British governments were unable to fill. However, while constitutional politics stagnated, the IRA had reorganized and some in the **Republican** movement were pressing for a more active role for Sinn Féin as a political party. There seemed little opportunity for any major impact to be made on the political stage as IRA atrocities, such as the La Mon restaurant bombing in which twelve **Protestants** were killed, angered many potential voters. In order for Republicanism to gain electoral support, a **catalyst** was needed to make **Nationalists** more radical.

Criminals or political prisoners?

Events in the **H-Blocks** of the Maze Prison were to provide that catalyst. Prior to 1976, anyone convicted of political offences was granted special category (political) status, with privileges such as being allowed to wear their own clothes. This changed when the Home Secretary declared that such prisoners would be treated as criminals and required to follow normal prison rules. IRA prisoners in the H-Blocks refused to accept this change: a long and tragic protest began.

The blanket protests

At first the protest took the form of a 'blanket' or 'dirty' protest. Prisoners refused to wear the prison uniforms, instead choosing to wear only blankets. Later they began to refuse to slop out toilet buckets, instead smearing the contents of the buckets over the walls of the cells. However, despite a concerted campaign by supporters of the prisoners there was no change in British policy

The H-blocks of the Maze Prison near Belfast.

and little sign of popular support. This changed in 1981 when the leader of the IRA in the Maze, Bobby Sands, began a **hunger strike** demanding the return of political status.

The hunger strike

Sands' decision provided an example and soon other Republican prisoners followed him on to hunger strike. They began to gain support from **Catholics** across Ireland, even those who previously had no sympathy for the IRA. The campaign accelerated when Sands stood, and was elected for, the parliamentary seat of Fermanagh-South Tyrone. Still Margaret Thatcher's government refused to concede to the demands, despite pressure from world opinion and Catholic Church leaders. Sands' death on 5 May 1981 brought 100,000 people on to the streets of Belfast for his funeral, but prompted no movement from the Prime Minister.

By August 1981, ten hunger strikers had died before pressure from relatives brought the protest to an end.

Gerry Adams helps carry the coffin of hunger striker Bobby Sands.

Two views of the prisoners' demands

'We are not prepared to consider special category status for certain groups of people serving sentences for crime. Crime is crime, it is not political.'
Margaret Thatcher, 21 April 1981

'I am a political prisoner because I am a casualty of a perennial war that is being fought between the oppressed Irish people and an alien ... regime that refuses to withdraw from our land.'
Bobby Sands, writing on the first day of his hunger strike

How did things change after the hunger strike?

The **hunger strike** and its aftermath had dramatic effects on the political situation in Northern Ireland. In the short term some of the prisoners' demands were granted on issues such as the right to wear their own clothes, concessions made only after the strikes were brought to an end. There was a dramatic increase in IRA violence, feeding off the popular support and anger generated by the strikers. This increase in violence led to an even greater gulf between **Protestants** and **Catholics**, the former bewildered at the rise in support for men they regarded as terrorists and murderers.

Internationally Northern Ireland had returned to the headlines. The suffering of the hunger strikers led to protests outside British embassies around the world. Union Jacks were burned in New York, where a visit by Prince Charles was met by anti **H-Block** campaigners, while in Le Mans, France, a street was named after Sands.

Thousands of people march in an anti-H-block demonstration through the streets of Belfast.

Sympathy for the demands of the hunger strikers and revulsion induced by their plight also led to the issue of Northern Ireland returning to the minds of many in the Republic of Ireland. The Irish and British governments were concerned at the startling rise of Sinn Féin and the increasing support for the IRA, bringing a realization that support for the moderate SDLP was in danger. As a result a closer working relationship developed between the two governments, ultimately resulting in the Anglo-Irish Agreement of 1985.

The rise of Sinn Féin

In the long term the hunger strike brought Sinn Féin a much greater share of **Nationalist** support. The hunger strikers were regarded as martyrs by some in the Nationalist community, and the election of Bobby Sands led many within **Republicanism** to realize the potential uses of **democracy**. The phrase 'with the ballot paper in one hand and the armalite [rifle] in the other' neatly summed up the new Republican strategy. It implied a continuation of violence with an attempt to increase support for Sinn Féin among the Catholic population. The 1983 election saw Gerry Adams returned as MP for West Belfast as the SDLP lost votes to Sinn Féin across the country. In 1973, the year after Bloody Sunday, Sinn Féin had gained only 3 per cent of the vote; ten years later that figure had risen to 13.4 per cent.

'Ten people had the courage to stand by their country to the point of dying for it. The H-Block issue became a worldwide issue. The Republican movement gained enormously in the number of people who joined, in favourable publicity and in finance.'
Daithi O'Conaill, Sinn Féin, December 1981

'When Bobby Sands died many of us felt its back to square one. If you tried to call a peace rally now you wouldn't get anyone to come.'
Mairead Corrigan, leader of a peace movement, December 1981

The Anglo-Irish Agreement

The growth in electoral support for Sinn Féin worried the British and Irish governments. They feared that this would threaten the more moderate SDLP, making it even more difficult to find a solution. Both governments were anxious to provide the SDLP with something that would give hope to the **Nationalist** community; that a United Ireland was an achievable goal.

The New Ireland Forum

The SDLP hoped that the Dublin government would provide support for the Nationalist community in the north. In the summer of 1983 the Irish government held a conference to discuss the future of Ireland. All the main Nationalist parties in Ireland attended, except Sinn Féin. **Unionists** refused to take part. In May 1984 it published three possible solutions to the conflict:

- A united Ireland
- A confederation of North and South
- Joint Authority by the British and Irish Governments.

Margaret Thatcher rejected the ideas.

The Grand Hotel, Brighton, after the attack on the Conservative Party Conference, 1984.

The Irish Taoiseach Garret Fitzgerald (left) and Margaret Thatcher at the signing of the Anglo-Irish Agreement.

The Anglo-Irish Agreement

In October 1984 the IRA bombed the Conservative Party Conference at Brighton. Several members of the party were killed, with the Prime Minister herself coming close to the blast. This brought the realities of the situation closer to the government who began secret talks with the Irish government. In November of 1984 the British and Irish Prime Ministers signed the Anglo-Irish Agreement at Hillsborough Castle.

The terms of the agreement were:
- The British government recognized that the Republic had the right to try to influence policy in Northern Ireland
- Both governments said they wanted to make Northern Ireland a place where people could 'live in peace, free from discrimination and intolerance'
- Both governments agreed to an inter-governmental conference, to discuss political measures, including security
- The Republic accepted that a united Ireland could only be implemented if Unionists agreed.

The SDLP welcomed the agreement hoping that it would provide them with something tangible to offer their voters but Sinn Féin rejected it, objecting to the Unionist veto of a united Ireland. To Sinn Féin, Ireland should be regarded as a united nation with a Unionist minority, and so their majority in Northern Ireland was not valid.

Unionist reaction

Unionists were furious, feeling that the agreement brought in the joint authority that Thatcher had rejected after the New Ireland Forum. They had not been consulted about the terms of the agreement and regarded it as a direct result of the SDLP's demands at the Forum. Protests were organized while **Loyalist paramilitaries** stepped up their campaigns. Increasingly the Loyalists turned against the **RUC** because they believed that the RUC was enforcing the agreement on the government's behalf.

Under the slogan '**Ulster** says NO', the main Unionist parties joined forces to organize huge protest rallies on the anniversary of the signing of the agreement in 1985 and 1986 but it became increasingly obvious that the government was not going to back down. There was no stomach within the Unionist community for a repeat of the Ulster Workers' strike of 1974 and gradually the protests began to disappear.

Results of the Agreement

- The British and Irish governments had shown that they were prepared to increase their co-operation in Northern Ireland.
- **Republicans**, despite their rejection of the agreement itself, began to realize that negotiation could bring results for the **Nationalist** community.
- Unionists and Loyalists felt increasingly isolated, realizing that the British government was prepared to put into place policies without consulting them and began to feel that they too would need to get involved in talks if they wanted to influence government policy.

Opposing reactions

'The Prime Minister signed away the Union at Hillsborough Castle ... We are at the window ledge of the Union ... That does not mean we are going to jump off.'
Peter Robinson, Deputy Leader of the DUP

'This deal does not go anywhere near bringing peace to this part of Ireland. On the contrary it reinforces **partition** because Dublin is recognizing Northern Ireland.'
Gerry Adams, President of Sinn Féin

Biography: the Reverend Ian Paisley

Ian Paisley has been a dominant figure in Northern Irish politics for over 30 years. As leader of the **Democratic** Unionist Party (DUP) he has resisted any agreements that he believed would allow the Irish **Republic** influence in Northern Ireland. As leader of the Free **Presbyterian** Church he has blended fundamentalist anti-**Catholic Protestantism** with his staunchly Unionist politics.

More moderate Unionist leaders, from Terence O'Neill to David Trimble, have been criticized and are wary of his ability to attract voters fearful of change. He opposed both the Power-sharing **Executive** of 1973 and the Anglo-Irish Agreement of 1985, and his party campaigned against the Good Friday Agreement in 1998. In doing so he has built up a sizeable and loyal following: he consistently tops the polls in elections to the European Parliament. However, critics argue that he has failed to provide any constructive alternative vision for Northern Ireland's future.

Ian Paisley addressing a rally against the Anglo-Irish Agreement.

Hopes for Peace

Talks about talks

After the signing of the Anglo-Irish Agreement, **Unionists** refused to meet with British Ministers. In September 1987, however, James Molyneaux, leader of the Official Unionist Party, and Ian Paisley, leader of the **Democratic** Unionist Party, agreed to engage in 'talks about talks'. Over the next four years many attempts were made to get the parties in Northern Ireland to hold meaningful talks but differences over the Anglo-Irish agreement prevented progress. In March 1991 the British and Irish inter-governmental conference was suspended to allow talks to take place outside the shadow of the agreement. The talks hoped to deal first with the internal government of Northern Ireland before discussing north-south and Anglo-Irish relations. However, the discussions never got past the first stage, so the Secretary of State, Peter Brooke, was forced to bring them to an end. The gulf between Unionists and **Nationalists** seemed as broad as ever.

The Hume-Adams initiative

In January of 1992 the Deputy President of Sinn Féin, Martin McGuinness, said that his party was willing to engage in talks with the British government. The government replied that it would only become involved in talks if there was a complete end to IRA violence. It is now known that secret talks between the two were held in 1992. In 1993, John Hume began talks with the Sinn Féin leader, Gerry Adams. These resulted in a document, known as the Hume-Adams initiative, being presented to both governments, although its contents were not made public.

Unionist reaction

Hume came in for a great deal of criticism from Unionists and some sections of the media. This heightened when the IRA exploded a bomb in a fish shop on the **Protestant** Shankill Road in Belfast: ten people were killed and Unionists were outraged when Adams carried the coffin of the bomber, who was also killed in the blast. Despite this Hume continued his meetings with Adams. There were further Unionist concerns about the secrecy surrounding the Hume-Adams proposals. They feared that the two were going to influence the British government while they were not consulted.

Hopes for peace in the 1990s were continually threatened by sporadic violence and bombings.

Biography: John Hume

John Hume first came to prominence in the **Civil Rights** movement during the late 1960s. He helped form the Social Democratic and Labour Party in 1970, becoming its leader in 1979 when he also became a Member of the European Parliament. He has been at the centre of many of the moves which have helped to shape Northern Ireland's political landscape. He was a member of the 1973 Power-sharing **Executive** and a force behind the Anglo-Irish Agreement of 1985 and his talks with Gerry Adams and influence in Irish America were instrumental in bringing about the Good Friday Agreement. He won the Nobel Peace Prize along with David Trimble. However, some critics argue that his efforts to bring Sinn Féin into the political arena have damaged relations with Unionists and the future of his own party.

John Hume, leader of the SDLP.

41

The Downing Street Declaration

Three months after the Hume-Adams proposals were handed over, the British and Irish governments issued a joint declaration on the future of Northern Ireland. They hoped their proposals would create the basis of trust and co-operation, which would allow the parties of Northern Ireland to meet and come to an agreement. The Downing Street Declaration was released on the 15 December 1993.

In the Declaration both governments agreed to try to implement 'a new political framework based upon consent' but that only parties who were committed to 'exclusively peaceful methods' could engage in talks. The British government declared that it had 'no selfish strategic or economic interest in Northern Ireland' (Britain had nothing to gain from its presence in Northern Ireland) and that a united Ireland was achievable through peaceful and **democratic** methods. In turn the Irish government agreed that a united Ireland would only be possible if the majority in Northern Ireland agreed. In the event of a cross-party agreement in the north they would amend their constitution to remove their claim over Northern Ireland.

John Major and Irish Taoiseach Albert Reynolds after agreeing the terms of the Downing Street Declaration in December 1993.

The declaration appeared to have something for everyone, **Unionists** had the guarantee that Northern Ireland's position within the UK would not be changed unless the majority of the population agreed, and **Nationalists** were promised that a united Ireland was achievable. However, not all were pleased: Ian Paisley declared that **Ulster** had been sold 'to buy off the fiendish **Republican** scum' and Sinn Féin was angry that the Irish government had agreed that a united Ireland would require the consent of the majority in the North. Despite this most parties welcomed the proposals. Pressure, especially from Irish-Americans, grew on Sinn Féin and the IRA to respond with a ceasefire. An opportunity for peace seemed to have arrived.

Biography: Gerry Adams

Gerry Adams has been a key figure behind the changes in Republican political strategy which led to their involvement in the peace process. Since the early 1970s he has held central positions within the Republican leadership. The security services believe he was an IRA leader before becoming President of Sinn Féin in 1983. He was arrested and interned for suspected IRA membership in 1971 but was released to be part of an IRA delegation which took part in secret talks with the British government in 1972. In 1979 he began to argue that

Gerry Adams, President of Sinn Féin.

military means alone would not lead to a united Ireland and argued for greater involvement in politics, a view supported by the increase in electoral support for Sinn Féin following the hunger strikes. In 1983 he became MP for West Belfast but refused to take his seat in Parliament at Westminster. His 1993 talks with John Hume were crucial to bringing about the first IRA ceasefire and he has been an important figure in persuading Republicans to accept the Good Friday Agreement.

The Media and the Conflict

The Northern Ireland Troubles have raged for 30 years in the full view of the world's media. This was not a war fought in the scrublands of Africa or mountains of Asia, but one fought on Europe's doorstep. The streets of Belfast and fields of South Armagh are easily accessible to the world's press, which has been accused of bias by both sides. The line between impartial news reporting and providing an opportunity for **paramilitary propaganda** has often been difficult to find.

The media in Northern Ireland

There are two major morning newspapers in Northern Ireland: the *Belfast Newsletter* and the *Irish News*. Traditionally the *Newsletter* is read by **Unionists** and the *Irish News* by **Nationalists** so not only are the two communities divided by their opinions but also the source of their information. One of the most surprising aspects of the peace process was the decision of the two papers to adopt a common, pro-agreement, approach, with each campaigning for a 'Yes' vote in the referendum. The evening newspaper, the *Belfast Telegraph*, is read by both communities and has found itself criticized by both sides who argue that it is either too Nationalist or too Unionist. On television, both *BBC Northern Ireland* and *Ulster Television* have been criticized for similar reasons.

Irish press reaction in the *Belfast Telegraph* to the events of Bloody Sunday, January 1972.

Reporting the conflict in Britain

The troubles have long been a controversial topic in the British media. Both newspapers and television producers have come under fire from one side or the other for their reporting on the conflict.

The national newspapers in Britain tend to follow the line of the British political party that they traditionally support. The *Daily Mail, Daily Express* and *Daily Telegraph,* for example, have generally supported the Conservative Party which is sympathetic to the Unionist case. They have been especially defensive of the army's role in Northern Ireland. The *Daily Mirror* and the *Guardian*, who tend to support the Labour Party, favour the Nationalists. All are opposed to paramilitary violence.

Daily Mail

MOUNTBATTEN SPECIAL ISSUE

MURDER OF LORD LOUIS

Mountbatten and 17 soldiers killed by IRA

Earl Mountbatten — murdered on an Irish holiday

Grim-faced helpers carry the body of Lord Mountbatten away from the harbour

British media outrage after the murder of the Queen's cousin Lord Louis Mountbatten, in August 1979.

The government's attitude: propaganda or censorship?

Throughout the troubles reporters have examined issues and stories that have proved awkward for the British government. The government has been accused of censoring television documentaries in order to cover up potentially embarrassing incidents. Its response has been to argue that some censorship is necessary both to safeguard the lives of security force personnel and to ensure that paramilitaries do not gain support and credibility. In 1977 the BBC 'This Week' programme examined the prisons issue, revealing the extent to which paramilitary prisoners were able to run their prison wings themselves. Two weeks later a prison officer who appeared in the programme was shot dead. Critics of the media's role in Northern Ireland seized on the case as evidence of the dangers caused by such reporting. The programme makers insisted that the officer's death was in no way connected to his appearance on 'This Week'.

The problem arose again in 1988 when ITV Thames produced the documentary 'Death on the Rock'. It examined the events leading up to the shooting of three IRA members in Gibraltar by the SAS. The three were planning to bomb a military band but were unarmed when they were shot. The programme claimed that no attempt was made to arrest the three victims, much to the government's fury as the official inquest into the events had not yet been heard.

Attempts to ban the programme failed and the subsequent enquiry supported much of what the makers had said. Soon after, the government announced legislation banning television producers from showing direct statements from representatives of Sinn Féin and the UDA. This resulted in actors providing a voice over for the statements in order to bypass the ban, which remained in place until the onset of the peace process.

A still from the Thames TV documentary 'Death on the Rock', showing the petrol station where three IRA members were shot by the SAS.

The Unionist view

Unionists believe that the British media is unduly sympathetic to Republicanism and tends to portray their own community in an unfavourable light. To Unionists, for example, the extensive coverage of the **hunger strikes** and the funerals which followed was little more than a **propaganda** coup for the IRA, failing to focus on the suffering of the Unionist community.

This feeling was heightened by the fact that bombs in English towns and cities were covered in greater depth than the regular atrocities carried out in Northern Ireland. The Broadcasting Ban of 1988 was welcomed by Unionists who felt that allowing representatives of **paramilitary** groups the opportunity to justify recent killings brought further suffering to the relatives of the victims.

The Nationalist view

Nationalists also criticize the mainstream British media, feeling that news reports failed to look at the underlying reasons for IRA violence or to fully examine killings carried out by British forces in Northern Ireland. The attempted censorship of those programme makers who tried to look into such issues further angered Nationalists and **Republicans**. Such criticism reached its height with the introduction of the Broadcasting Ban on Sinn Féin members, with Nationalists arguing that many were elected representatives who had a right and a duty to give their opinion.

The problems faced by the media in attempting to explain the situation in Northern Ireland and to examine controversial topics are clear. They must be wary that they do not add fuel to already tense situations or provide opportunities for propaganda. At the same time they have an important role to play in ensuring that people have the opportunity to hear both sides of the story. In doing so they allow greater understanding of the complex issues which surround a conflict such as that in Northern Ireland. Attempted censorship can be counterproductive, attracting greater publicity to a programme and raising questions as to why it is being censored.

The Peace Process

On 31 August 1994 the IRA announced a complete cessation of violence. The **Loyalist paramilitaries** followed on 13 October. Both groups hoped that an end to violence would allow the political leaders to meet to discuss a settlement. This was not immediately the case. There was concern among **Unionists** that the IRA ceasefire was merely a tactic that brought no guarantees of permanence. They were unwilling to enter into talks with Sinn Féin under these circumstances and the British government was unable to persuade them. Meanwhile the **Republican**s grew restless waiting for their representatives to reach the talks table.

The Framework document

In an effort to prevent the peace collapsing, the two government's issued 'Frameworks for the Future' in which they outlined their vision of a possible settlement. In Part I of the document they suggested an assembly of 90 members elected under **proportional representation**. Three members would jointly chair the assembly that would have responsibility for matters such as health, education and agriculture. Part II gave plans for north-south bodies which would have 'executive, harmonizing and consultative functions.' The role of these bodies was open to 'progressive extension, by agreement, of its functions to new areas,' aiming towards 'greater integration'.

Unionists were furious: to them the 'executive functions' of the north-south bodies, and 'progressive extension' of these functions, meant the creeping introduction of a united Ireland. In August, James Molyneaux was forced to resign as leader of the UUP, having claimed to have assurances from the British government that this would not be the case. David Trimble replaced him in September.

The weapons issue

Unionists argued that Republicans had not shown their commitment to purely peaceful methods as they still held on to their weapons. **Decommissioning** of these weapons, they said, must take place before the talks. Republicans refused, saying that any decommissioning would only come after a settlement had been agreed.

Biography: David Trimble

David Trimble, who won the Nobel Peace prize along with John Hume in 1998, began his political career in William Craig's hard-line Vanguard party in the 1970s. In 1978 he joined the **Ulster** Unionist Party, becoming an MP in 1990, before becoming the surprise choice as party leader in 1995. He had come to prominence during the Drumcree marching dispute where he was seen to work alongside Ian Paisley, so many observers were surprised when he soon travelled south to meet with political leaders in the Irish Republic. He led his party into the negotiations leading to the Good Friday Agreement and campaigned for its acceptance in the **referendum** which followed. Since then he has been elected First Minister of Northern Ireland but has faced difficulties in maintaining his party's support for the Assembly. The lack of movement on the decommissioning issue has led to several challenges to both his party leadership and the UUP's position in the Assembly.

David Trimble, Northern Ireland's First Minister and leader of the Ulster Unionists.

In an attempt to kick-start the process, an American Senator, George Mitchell, was called in to look into the issue. His report was delivered on 24 January 1996, and suggested that decommissioning should take place during the talks. Other 'confidence-building measures' should also be put in place. **Punishment beatings** should be stopped and elections could be held to determine the strengths of the parties before talks would begin. John Major, the British Prime Minister, agreed and announced plans for elections.

The end of the ceasefires

The IRA believed that too much was being asked of them. To them the ceasefire itself was a major concession and Sinn Féin had the right to take part in talks regardless of weapons and elections. On 4 February 1996 they exploded a huge bomb near Canary Wharf in London, killing two people. A year of violence followed before another opportunity to achieve a peace settlement was brought about.

The second IRA ceasefire

On 1 May 1997 John Major's Conservative Party was defeated in the British general election and Tony Blair replaced him as Prime Minister, leading the Labour government. Mo Mowlam became Secretary of State for Northern Ireland and it was soon announced that talks with Sinn Féin would take place.

Three months later, on 19 July a second ceasefire was announced by the IRA, on the understanding that this would be enough to allow Sinn Féin into the talks, regardless of the **decommissioning** issue. This time David Trimble was able to persuade the **Unionist** Party to set aside their concerns and enter into the talks. However, Ian Paisley and the DUP refused to take part, providing a rallying point for future Unionist opposition.

The Good Friday Agreement

The winter of 1997 and early 1998 brought difficulties for the talks. Both the UFF and IRA breached their ceasefires and saw their political representatives suspended from the talks. Senator George Mitchell, the American Chairman of the talks, realized that a deadline would be necessary to focus the minds of those involved and decided on Good Friday 1998. All parties agreed and the talks continued but with little sign of movement until the arrival of the Irish and British Prime Ministers the night before the deadline. All-night talks followed and by 5.30 on the Friday afternoon, agreement had been reached.

For the first time Unionists and **Republicans** had agreed upon a programme for running Northern Ireland, and stated that they were willing to work together to ensure its success. A **referendum** was planned on both sides of the border to demonstrate public support.

The terms of the Agreement

The Good Friday Agreement has far reaching consequences for Northern Ireland, covering issues as wide-ranging as safeguards for the Irish language and employment **legislation**. However, its main terms are as follows:

- A united Ireland could not be brought about without the consent of the people of Northern Ireland
- The Constitution of the Republic of Ireland would be changed to remove the claim over Northern Ireland
- A 108-member Assembly would be created which would have 10 departments; parties would be allocated departments according to their strength in the assembly; a First Minister and Deputy would be elected
- A North-South Ministerial Council was to be created with members from the Assembly and the Irish Parliament; it would meet to deal with issues of a mutual interest, such as tourism and fisheries
- Human Rights legislation was to be introduced with a Commission to ensure it was put into practice
- The **RUC** was to be reformed in an attempt to gain greater support from the **Catholic** community
- **Paramilitary** prisoners were to be released
- All parties agreed to work to try to achieve decommissioning.

American Senator George Mitchell was a key figure in the peace talks.

Reaction to the Agreement

Around the world there was a collective sigh of relief at the announcement, but in Northern Ireland the situation was not so clear. Ian Paisley argued for a 'No' vote in the **referendum** which followed. His supporters pointed out that, while the **RUC** was to be changed and prisoners released, there were no guarantees on the **decommissioning** issue. Furthermore, they claimed, the North-South Council was a first step towards a united Ireland.

However, most **Unionists** were not convinced by his arguments, including the **Loyalist paramilitaries**. As with the Anglo-Irish agreement, there would be no re-run of the 1974 Workers Strike. In the referendum which followed 71 per cent of the Northern Irish people voted in favour of the agreement, although Paisley was able to claim substantial support among Unionists. In the Republic 94 per cent agreed to accept the proposals and remove the constitutional claims over the North. Plans were put in place to put the agreement into action, with elections for the Assembly held in June.

Putting the Agreement into action

The Assembly met for the first time on 1 July 1998, electing David Trimble as First Minister with Seamus Mallon of the SDLP as his Deputy. However, a year later, when the British Government was due to hand over power to the Assembly, Trimble's Unionists refused to enter the **devolved** government. They argued that Sinn Féin and the IRA had failed to fulfil their obligation to begin decommissioning, and so they should be excluded from office. Sinn Féin, on the other hand, said that they had agreed to try to influence the IRA but nothing more. Stalemate had been reached yet again.

In November, however, the IRA agreed to appoint a representative to discuss decommissioning. Despite opposition from some hard-liners Trimble was able to persuade his party to go into the devolved **Executive** with Sinn Féin. Their continued involvement depended upon the IRA beginning decommissioning early in 2000. On 29 November the Executive was formed with representatives of Unionism, Nationalism and Republicanism sharing power for the first time. Trimble was at its head with a diverse team, including Sinn Féin's Martin McGuinness as Minister for Education and Peter Robinson, of the anti-agreement DUP, as Minister for Regional Development.

Problems remained: there was no movement from the IRA so the British Government was forced to suspend the Executive nine weeks later as Trimble threatened to withdraw. The IRA pulled out of disarmament talks soon after.

In the weeks that followed there was some movement from both sides. Trimble announced he was willing to return to the Executive if he was given firm guarantees that decommissioning would occur, and the IRA responded saying that it would 'completely and verifiably' put its arms beyond use. If Trimble and the **Ulster** Unionist Party agreed that this concession was enough – the IRA has not promised to get rid of its weapons, only to place them in secure arms dumps – the Executive could be reinstated. On 27 May Trimble was successful in persuading his party to accept the IRA offer, but only by the narrowest of margins: 459 delegates (53.2 %) supported him; 403 (46.8 %) voted against. On 5 June Assembly members returned to Stormont with the Executive back in place, power had been restored to Northern Ireland, but with many issues still waiting to be resolved.

Obstacles to peace

Weapons – Decommissioning has been a constant problem in the peace process. In the Good Friday Agreement itself the issue was 'fudged', Unionists could claim that it was a requirement; **Republicans** argued that it was something that could only be hoped for. To Unionists it is vital. They are mistrustful of the IRA and its reasons for involvement in the peace process. They point out that the first IRA ceasefire was brought to an end with violence when it seemed that the tide was going against the Republicans and they fear that this will happen again. Republicans argue that destroying weapons would be like admitting surrender and that it is more important that the guns remain silent.

Parades – The annual marching season brings tension to Northern Ireland. The annual **Orange Order** parade at Drumcree near Portadown has been the focal point for violence since 1995. What was once a country road now passes a **Nationalist** housing estate whose residents object to the parade and its symbolism. The Orangemen argue that it is a route they have marched for almost 200 years and they should be allowed to continue. The parade has become a focal point for Unionists angry at what they perceive to be the removal of their British culture from Northern Ireland and has seen violent stand offs with police each July.

The policing issue – The policing of Northern Ireland has always been a cause of conflict. Many **Nationalists** regard the **RUC** as a **Protestant** force which has been used to protect Unionism, and as such they felt unable to join or support it. **Unionists** argue that a quarter of the force's members were **Catholic** at the onset of the troubles and that it was IRA attacks and intimidation that discouraged Catholic members, rather than the culture of the RUC itself.

In the Good Friday Agreement it was accepted that changes had to be made to the RUC to ensure that Nationalists could give it their full support. Many Unionists were angered by the resulting reforms especially the proposal to change the force's name and insignia. Like the Parades issue they regard it as an erosion of the 'Britishness' of Northern Ireland. They also feel it is an insult to those RUC members who died or were injured in the troubles. Many Nationalists regard the changes as essential to building a new police force they can accept. Even the very name Royal **Ulster** Constabulary represents a force that they feel was biased against them throughout the troubles.

The Orange Order on parade at Drumcree. In recent years controversy over the march has led to violence and tension during the summer months.

Violence – Despite the ceasefires of the main **paramilitary** groups there has been sporadic violence which threatens to bring about a return to full-scale conflict. Many paramilitaries were unhappy with the new direction their leaderships took them, feeling that it betrayed old principles and would not bring about their aims.

This feeling was clearly demonstrated when a dissident Republican group calling themselves the Real IRA exploded a bomb in Omagh, Co. Tyrone in August 1998, killing 29 people. At the time there was a feeling of optimism in the country in the wake of the Good Friday Agreement; the Omagh bomb brought back the harsh realities of the conflict. Other attacks by both sides have followed, as paramilitary groups on both sides 'flex their muscles', but have thus far failed to deflect the politicians from their attempts to reach a settlement.

'We have seen 16 members of the Roman Catholic faith buried, one member of the Mormon faith and 11 members of the Protestant faith. Today we feel for them no matter what their beliefs or their personal politics are.'
Reverend Ian Paisley at the funeral of Esther Gibbon, killed in the Omagh bomb

The aftermath of the Omagh bombing. Dissident paramilitary groups remain a threat to the peace process.

Counting the Cost: Thirty Years of War

The violence that devastated Northern Ireland for so many years has inevitably left deep wounds within the **province**. There are few families who have not been affected in some way. Over 3500 people have been killed with thousands more injured. When the bombings and shootings of the troubles are reported, the names of the dead are reported, along with the number of injured. It often goes unnoticed that these injured may have been crippled for life. When the Abercorn Bar in Belfast was bombed in 1972 two sisters shopping for a wedding dress both lost their legs.

There are innumerable stories of violence and suffering from the conflict, too many for a book of this nature. One week in 1993 that had a devastating effect on two close-knit communities must stand as an example. On 23 October two IRA men walked into a fish shop on the **Protestant** Shankill Road in Belfast. They hoped to plant a bomb that would kill UDA members they

Thirty years of terrorism has shattered the business life of Northern Ireland, making it one of the worst unemployment black-spots in the United Kingdom.

believed were meeting upstairs. There was no meeting and the bomb exploded prematurely, killing nine Protestant civilians and one of the bombers. The youngest victim was a seven-year-old girl. Fifty-seven people were injured, including a 79-year-old woman and two baby boys. One of the paramedics described the scene. 'There was one lady lying in the road with head injuries and half her arm blown off. She later died. But the worst part for me was when we unearthed the body of a young girl. I will never forget that face staring up out of the rubble.'

One week later members of the UFF walked into the Rising Sun Bar in Greysteel. It was the night before Halloween and the bar was packed with 200 people, many in fancy dress. One of the masked gunmen shouted 'Trick or Treat' and many customers thought it was just a sick joke. Seconds later they opened fire, killing six **Catholics** and one Protestant, and leaving 19 others injured. The oldest victim was 81, the youngest just 19. Soon after, the husband of one of the victims, a 59-year-old mother of six, described what he saw. 'We went out on a Saturday night for a wee dance and they blew her to bits … I saw the gun coming round the corner and then I heard the bangs. My wife and friends were on the floor. They blew the legs off her. They shot her through the heart, through the back.'

The economic cost

The bombings and shootings of the troubles have not only destroyed lives, but also the economic stability of Northern Ireland. The province has the highest unemployment rate in the United Kingdom. Firms have been unwilling to invest in such an unstable area and explosions have destroyed town centres. Thus, many areas of Northern Ireland suffer from high levels of poverty and social deprivation.

The troubles have also been an immense drain on the British economy. One of the main reasons for the high levels of IRA violence was their desire to make Northern Ireland so costly to the British that they would aim to leave. In the 1970s it was estimated that the daily cost of terrorism was £500,000. Maintaining troop levels, compensation for victims and attempting to rejuvenate the Northern Ireland economy have all been costly. When the IRA ended its 1995 ceasefire with the huge bomb at Canary Wharf in London, £85 million worth of damage was done.

The troubles and young people

Young people in Northern Ireland have grown up in an atmosphere of tension and violence. It is still possible for young people in Northern Ireland to grow up never having met someone from the other community. Others have had relatives killed or wounded or have witnessed horrific incidents. In some cases these have left mental scars that may never heal.

The Good Friday Agreement may offer a hope of peace to the people of Northern Ireland but it will be many years before the bitterness and mistrust of thirty years of war is washed away. Political agreement is just the first step on the way to a better future for Northern Ireland.

The breakdown of law and order has led many young people to get involved in violence.

'*Sectarianism lives in us all – it is in the choices we make, it is in the words we say, it is even in the friends we make. It lives in our churches and it taints our community life. It makes possible the violent actions which we abhor.*'
Minister conducting the funeral of Elizabeth O'Neill, a Protestant married to a Catholic who was killed by a Loyalist bomb thrown into her home in June 1999

'*To see him lying there with half his head gone and those beautiful green eyes looking out at me as if he was waiting for me was devastating. I never realized how green his eyes were. The image will stay with me for the rest of my life.*'
The mother of James Barker, a twelve-year old boy killed by the Omagh Bomb in August 1998

Table 1: Responsibility for deaths 1966–1999

Year	Republicans	Loyalists	All security forces	Other	Total
1966	0	3	0	0	3
1967	0	0	0	0	0
1968	0	0	0	0	0
1969	5	3	10	0	18
1970	21	1	5	1	28
1971	107	22	46	5	180
1972	280	121	86	9	496
1973	137	90	32	4	263
1974	149	131	17	6	303
1975	130	121	7	9	267
1976	163	127	16	2	308
1977	74	28	7	7	116
1978	62	10	12	4	88
1979	104	18	2	1	125
1980	58	14	9	5	86
1981	84	14	17	2	117
1982	85	15	12	0	112
1983	62	12	11	2	87
1984	51	10	11	0	72
1985	47	2	5	4	58
1986	41	17	6	2	66
1987	74	20	10	2	106
1988	69	23	13	0	105
1989	57	19	2	3	81
1990	52	20	11	1	84
1991	53	41	6	2	102
1992	42	39	9	1	91
1993	39	48	0	3	90
1994	27	38	1	3	69
1995	7	2	0	0	9
1996	14	5	2	1	22
1997	5	13	1	2	21
1998	37	17	1	2	57
1999	3	3	0	0	6
Total	2139	1047	367	83	3636

Table 2: Victims of the troubles

Type of Person	Number
Civilians	2064
All security forces	1036
All paramilitaries	536
Total	3636

Source: *Lost Lives – The stories of the men, women and children who died as a result of the troubles,* by McKittrick, Kelters, Feeney and Thornton. Mainstream, Edinburgh, 1999.

Appendix
Chronology of events

1967 Northern Ireland Civil Rights Association (NICRA) set up

1968 Civil Rights campaign intensifies, leading Prime Minister Terrence O'Neill to propose reforms

1969 *February* O'Neill suffers heavy losses in general election, but presses on with his plans.
August serious rioting breaks out in Londonderry, with police beginning to lose control of situation. British army sent in to restore order.

1970 SDLP formed.

1971 First British soldier killed by IRA.
UDA formed.
DUP set up by Ian Paisley.

1972 Bloody Sunday: British army kill 13 Civil Rights marchers in Derry.
Direct Rule from London introduced.
Bloody Friday, IRA bombs kill 9 in Belfast city centre.

1973 Sunningdale Agreement sets up Power-sharing Executive

1974 Ulster Workers' Strike brings about collapse of Executive.
IRA bombing campaign in England intensifies.

1975 INLA set up

1976 Blanket protest by IRA prisoners begins

1979 IRA assassinate Queen's cousin, Lord Mountbatten, also killing 19 soldiers on same day in separate explosion

1981 Hunger strikes begin, eventually leading to deaths of 10 Republican prisoners

1983 New Ireland Forum set up in Dublin to discuss possible solutions to 'troubles'

1984 IRA bomb explodes at Conservative Party Conference in Brighton, killing 5

1985 Anglo-Irish Agreement signed giving Irish Republic some say in government of Northern Ireland

1986 Unionist protests against Anglo-Irish Agreement reach their height, with many Loyalist attacks on members of RUC

1987 IRA bomb kills 11 Protestant civilians attending Remembrance Day ceremony in Enniskillen.
'Talks about talks' begin.

1991 Inter-party talks finally get under way, but meet with no success

1992 Contact between the British government and Sinn Féin begins.
UDA banned as Loyalist violence by its offshoot, the UFF, increases.

1993 SDLP leader, John Hume, and Gerry Adams of Sinn Féin increase contacts, leading to Hume-Adams document.
IRA kills 10 Protestants in fish shop on Shankill Road in Belfast; wave of Loyalist violence follows, including gun attack in Greysteel, Co. Londonderry in which 8 die.

1994 *August* IRA ceasefire announced.
September Loyalists follow a month later.
Sinn Féin and British Government hold first official meetings.

1995 Framework Document produced by British and Irish governments, revealing plans for future arrangements in Northern Ireland.
July first of annual confrontations between Orange Marchers, police and Nationalist residents' groups at Drumcree near Portadown.

US President Bill Clinton visits Northern Ireland in attempt to boost peace process.

1996 IRA ceasefire ends with bomb at Canary Wharf in London as talks break down

1997 Despite rising tension IRA announces second ceasefire.
David Trimble leads his party into direct negotiations with Sinn Féin and Tony Blair becomes first Prime Minister to meet with a Sinn Féin leader since the 1920s.

1998 Good Friday Agreement concluded.
Referendum shows clear majority in favour.
Elections held to the new assembly.
August Dissident Republicans opposed to agreement kill 29 people in bomb explosion in Omagh, Co. Tyrone.
John Hume and David Trimble awarded Nobel Peace Prize.

1999 Unionists withdraw from Assembly as IRA decommissioning has not begun.
Trimble able to persuade party to return later in year.

2000 Lack of movement on decommissioning forces British government to suspend Assembly before second Unionist withdrawal.
IRA announces it will put its arms 'beyond use'.
Trimble again persuades Unionists to return to Assembly and Executive is restored.

Suggested reading

Lost Lives. The stories of the men women and children who died as a result of the Northern Ireland Troubles, by McKittrick, Kelters, Feeney, Thornton – Edinburgh: Mainstream Publishing, 1999

Provos – London, Bloomsbury 1998
Loyalists – London, Bloomsbury 2000
Brits – London, Bloomsbury 2001
All above by Peter Taylor, examining the roles of the IRA, Loyalist paramilitaries and British Army in the troubles. Good for eyewitness accounts.

Useful websites

http://news.bbc.co.uk
BBC news website
http://www.uup.org
The Ulster Unionist Party
http://www.indigo.ie/sdlp
The Social Democratic and Labour Party

http://www.sinnfein.ie
Sinn Fein
http://www.ni_assembly.gov.uk
The Northern Ireland Assembly

Glossary

Anglican a member of the Church of Ireland, which is part of the worldwide Anglican church. Also called Episcopalian in the US.

Apprentice Boys A Protestant association set up in 1814 to commemorate the part played by the Apprentice Boys in the Seige of Derry

B-Specials a reserve police force, almost entirely Protestant, called into service in times of civil conflict

catalyst an event which sparks change

Catholic a member of the Roman Catholic Church

census an official survey of the population

civil rights the rights of individual citizens supported by law; relating to jobs, housing, voting rights and the legal system

colony a territory ruled by another state; usually the people of the colony have no political power and are ruled for the economic benefit of the other state

consultative body a group of politicians from both sides of the border who meet to make suggestions for policy in Northern Ireland

decommissioning the destruction of illegal, paramilitary weapons

democracy, democratic a form of government where people exercise power through voting; the majority vote is accepted as the decision

devolve transfer power to a lower level; e.g. to transfer power from central government to local government

executive a branch of government that introduces and enforces laws

gerrymander drawing up electoral boundaries so that they suit one political group; it ensures that political opponents are concentrated in one area, so have less representatives

H-blocks a name given to the Maze Prison, where many Loyalist and Republican paramilitaries were jailed; the buildings at the Maze had a distinctive 'H' shape

hunger strike a protest against prison conditions organized by Republican prisoners; the protesters refused to accept any food

legislation discussing and making laws

Loyalist a member of the Unionist community who is prepared to use or support violence to support the union with Britain

militant favouring violent or confrontational action in support of a cause

Nationalist someone who hopes to achieve a united Ireland through peaceful, political methods

Orange Order a Protestant organization which commemorates the victory of King William of Orange at the battle of the Boyne in July 1690; formed in 1795 to defend Protestant and Unionist interests in Ireland

paramilitary a member of an illegal organization that is prepared to use violence, such as the IRA or UVF

partition the division of Ireland into two separate states in 1921: the Irish Free State and Northern Ireland

planters Protestant immigrants from Scotland and England who were brought to Ulster in the 17th century by King James I

Presbyterian a member of the Protestant Presbyterian Church

propaganda information that is biased or designed to mislead

proportional representation an electoral system allowing voters to choose candidates in a descending order of preference; minority parties are more able to gain representation under this system

Protestant a member of a church which is separated from the Roman Catholic Church, and follows the principles of the reformation

province an old administrative area in Ireland; there are four provinces - Ulster, Munster, Leinster and Connaught; the province of Ulster has 9 counties, 3 of which – Donegal, Cavan and Monaghan – are not part of Northern Ireland

punishment beatings vicious attacks carried out by members of paramilitary groups upon their own communities for what are termed 'anti-social' crimes, such as car theft, burglary and drug dealing

referendum a general vote by the people to show opinion on a subject

repeal to revoke or declare something invalid

republic a state in which power is held by the general people who elect a leader

Republican a member of the Nationalist community who is prepared to use or support the use of violence to gain a united Ireland

Royal Ulster Constabulary (RUC) the police force of Northern Ireland

sectarian concerning actions or attitudes based on membership of a group or community

socialist someone who believes in a society run by and benefiting the people

Taoiseach the prime minister of the Republic of Ireland

Ulster an ancient province of Ireland

Unionist someone in favour of keeping Northern Ireland's links with Britain and believes in using peaceful methods to achieve this